Ascendant

Kassandra Olschanski

to the people who stuck around

DEAR READER,

i was on a train to chicago in the summer of 2016 when i wrote my first poem. at this time i had gone through my first very minor heartbreak and a lesson i have learned in many different occasions since then is that sometimes we do not get the closure we want from people, so we have to make it ourselves.

i found the answers i needed from writing my thoughts down and coming from someone who keeps everything inside, i needed to do this.

in the process of making some of the best memories ever of the course of these past three years, i also dealt with a lot of loss, depression and anxiety. this was a time in my life where i was at my lowest points for a consistent amount of time. i stopped believing in getting better, i was convinced my life would only get worse.

i managed to hit rock bottom and kept digging myself down, i thought there was never a way i could rise up from here.

i recently found myself again in a trip i took to new york city. maybe this is what flipped the switched for me, maybe it was the time i spent with my friends. but i came back from that trip feeling like i could breathe again for the first time in three years. i did a lot of thinking and i realized that this world is too big for me to feel this small. i looked back on where i was three years ago and who i am today and all the growth i have had and i am proud of who i have become. healing is a process and sometimes there are setbacks, low points, loss and heartbreaks, and if there is anything i have learned these past couple of years is that it will get better (i was told that by someone very special.. if you know you know).

the point being, i thought the only thing i had left in this life was bad days and i was so wrong. i am so much stronger than i ever thought i could be.

i decided to name this book Ascendant because by definition Ascendant means "rising in power" which is how i have felt lately for the first time in a few years. i felt like i finally grabbed back all the power i had lost, and i felt myself rising up again after i hit rock bottom.

there is no one where to go but up.

all my love,
kassandra

you never knew i was a writer
so you have no idea
that i am writing this now

if i was a flower
i would want to be a sunflower
tall and golden
shining brighter than
the sun herself

i love the feeling
after you swim in waves all day
and you lay down to sleep at night
and you can still feel them
like i can still feel you
after all this time

look at you
you managed to break someone
who was already broken

- how did you do that

the first time you saw me watch the sky
was that night in july
it is january now and the sky seems to look
just the same as it did that night
as if nothing has changed
oh but it has
not the way i admire the sky
but the way i would admire you

i do admit
i miss your kiss
but i do not miss
your lying lips

i have always admired the ocean
almost just as much as i admired you
the waves come and go
just as you do
but the one thing i found in the ocean was comfort
and i could never seem to find that in you

you loved outer space
but unfortunately for me
i was a star that did not burn
quite bright enough
for you to love

they have spent so much time
trying to tear you down
trying to attack your character
for every little thing that you do
people are hard to please
and maybe the real problem is
we can never please them all
so the best things to do
is to stick to the ones who know you
the ones that really know you
the ones that never left your side
even when things got hard
i have always had your back
like you have always had mine

- for t.s

you told me i deserved better than you
maybe you were all i ever needed
but you decided
i was better off
without even asking me

- i make my own decisions

i guess i thought maybe
i could be your favorite flower
so i thought you picked me because of that
but i was wrong

- you should have left me to grow

you spend time admiring planets
stars and galaxies
you took some time to admire me too
i was the brightest star in the galaxy
until you almost put my light out
but i took some time
and the girl you admired
is still here
burning brighter than ever
without you

you talked me into your future
then kicked me to your past
funny how you did that so fast

i had a dream that you called me
just to talk
what a sight that would be
to see you calling me
just because you missed me

the thing i love about us
is we are the type of people
to stay awake until the sun rises
that is just what we do
we stay awake, until the sun is awake
the sad part of this is
we will never be staying awake
for the same sunrise

- distance

they will try to tell you
that speaking up does not work
or that your actions for change
are being done just because you want attention
they will tell you that you are being dramatic
or that you are too young to understand
but let me tell you a little secret
the reason they are trying so hard to stop you
is because these things work
it is in the history

- never underestimate our marches

maybe the best thing for you to do
is to take a step back
look in the mirror
and realize
that everyone else
can not really be the problem
now can they?

if you were to look at my search history
you would find questions
asking how many pills
of the medication i have
would be enough
to just make it all stop

- the worst week of my life

the tears streamed down my face
on more than one occasion
you came to my rescue
time and time again
thank you for giving me strength

- to my mom

the best feeling
was to look up
and see a sky full of stars
and just know that
your biggest dreams
were about to come true

- friday night in texas

i am made up of starlight
and i will not apologize
for your lack
of being able to see that

- you missed a shooting star

are you not satisfied
until you have a new girl
wrapped around your finger
every waking day?

i have spent so many nights
picking myself up
after crying on the bathroom floor
because if we are being honest
the only person you can really count on
is yourself

why do i get mad at myself
when i choose myself
this does not happen often
but the times i put myself first
i feel like that is the wrong choice
and that my time should not be spent bettering myself
i spend most of my time catering to others
the people i am surrounded by
have no problem choosing themselves
in almost every conversation we have
and that is fine
but am i the only one who feels guilty
in spending time saving myself
when the time could be spent saving someone else

- still learning how to care for myself too

111 miles
is the distance from me to you
i would have done anything to get rid of that distance
just to be with you

dreams they bring back
those faces of your past
that you would really rather forget

i spent so much time
convincing myself that the way i am was wrong
and i should change that
but i now take pride in the fact
that i am not the type of person
who is self-involved
i always battled with myself
on being more open with people and be more willing to share things
and i know there is a fine line with this
it is not so black-and-white
and not everything is so simple
but i would rather let others show me their happiness
than make someone feel as if their experiences do not matter
which is how you made me feel

- how you made all of us feel

it is the oldest trick in the book
the minute you are happy without them
is the minute they finally show up

i learned at a very young age
to shove the way i feel back down my throat
before i ever even got the chance to say anything
because no one really cares anyway

- no wonder i can not breathe

we grew up together
which is something i can not say about anyone else
we have spent enough nights crying to fill a whole ocean
and enough nights spent in ice cream shops
and days spent with a smashed watermelon in the grass
because we needed to get our anger out
our childhood looks like splattered paint
of all different colors on the floor
and nights surrounded by the lights of tiki torches and sparklers
i know timing is never the best for you
actually your timing is always the worst
but when we became friends
your timing was the best
the distance is scary
london is too many miles away
but the further you go
the stronger our hearts grow
there is so much i can say
but let you remind you of this
everything is going to be okay
everything will work out in the end

- best friends since forever

i have to remind myself
that i can stay upset
for as long as i need to
to be able to heal
i have trained myself to swallow anything
and everything that i am feeling
and get over it and move past it
but i am tired of doing that
i am going to feel everything i need to feel
for as long as i need to feel it

your magic and the power
you put into all of your work
is wonderful and enchanting
and the way you are able to
radiate who you are in your art
is the most inspirational thing
i have ever seen in my life

- for xcx

i remember the anger in my finger tips
as i pushed the door open to leave
the thought of you spending your time
with someone else
was just enough to push me over the edge
and i do not know why
it is not like you never tried to give us a try

- i know i am to blame for this one

you are the type of person
to make everyone
feel bad
for doing absolutely
nothing wrong

i remember i tried to distract you
i asked you to look at the sky
instead of me but you could not take your eyes off me
but now i wish that was still the case
because very quickly
you got sick of looking at me

- i will be careful what i ask for next time

i do not understand the point
in making all of your friends wonder
if you actually still want to be friends with them
or not

- friendship is meant to be easy

you believed in me
when i did not believe in myself
you saw the light
when all i could see is the darkness
i do not think there was a bad time
that ever passed by
where you were never there for me
you were always right by my side

"well i mean you'll never know."

i guess i won't

there is no excuse
no explanation
no reason
for your friends to not be there for you
in the times when you need it the most
i remember searching my mind to try
and figure out why one of my friends was
unable to be there for me
in one of the hardest times
i shrugged my shoulders
as that is just life
and then one year later
i realized it is not just life
as a vase full of flowers
and a weighted blanket
was delivered to my door
from my real friends
who were doing everything they could
to let me know that i always have and always will
have an army behind me
and it was them
they were there for me
they cared
it is as simple as that

- real friends

i would give anything
to have a normal mind
i would give anything
to wake up without struggle
i would give anything
to walk outside without worry
i would give anything
to go to school without any hesitation
i would give anything to be able to work
and have normal hours
i would give anything
to know what it is like to breathe
i would give anything
to know what it is not like to not shake
i would give anything to just be able to function
i would give anything
for the small things in life
to just be easy

a sisterhood that was like no other
filled with many polaroids
and butterflies that were blue
coffee shops and trips to toronto
there was dancing in the rain
and many wine filled nights
we lift each other up
and never let each other down

- a duo that was incredible

one of the biggest tragedies in life
is watching a friendship fall apart
right in front of your eyes

i think about you a lot
you appear in my dreams
sometimes i wonder
what we could have been
if we gave it a chance
before i left too soon

a girl broke your heart
so maybe i was just
that girl in between
the girl you used
to pass your time
until the new girl you wanted
actually came by

- but i was not the girl you wanted

but even the beautiful sunrise
could not distract me
from those eyes

i could have been your angel
but you decided my taste of heaven
just was not for you

- have fun in hell

there is so much
i never got to say
and honestly
maybe it is better off this way

- july 28th

flowers are only meant
to bloom for such a short time
i knew we were just like the flowers
and i tried to preserve us
as people do
when they press flowers in a book
but we died off
just as flowers always do

you grabbed my hand
and i tightened my grip
and i held on
but then
you suddenly
and very quickly
let go of me

we had plans to watch alice in wonderland
and i bet you still have not seen that damn movie
to this day

- wonderland was always my thing anyway

i have been trying to convince myself
to still see the best in you
even though you showed me
the absolute worst in you

i battled with this
in my mind for so long
and then i realized
i needed to stop convincing myself
of one thing and then realizing
i might be convincing myself of the wrong thing
i just decided to let it be
because what will be will be
it is not as big of a deal as they all make it seem
at least not to me

i have grown sick and tired
of being the girl
guys only want temporarily
i am the girl they use to make their lonely nights
pass by just a bit quicker
the one comes after their ex
but before their new lover
no one ever wants me enough to stay
i am always just temporary

honestly
i should have known
that when i was letting go of your hand
i was letting go of you too

i guess you did not want to know me
and that is fine
i can not make you want to know me
but what was the purpose
for stringing me along
for as long as you did

the situation is simple
when it comes to friends
there is always going to be a point
in which we notice that maybe
someone who we call our friend
is not actually our friend
and this is a hard realization
the good side to this is
when your world is crashing down
and after the fake friends fan out
the true friends are there standing tall
and burning brighter than ever

- if you are my real friend, thank you

i am tired of ambulances sirens
and phone calls that only bring
the sign of death

if you want to erase me from your life
i will erase you from mine
but we really know which one of us
is at a loss here
and it is not me my dear

fall was always my favorite season
until three fall seasons in a row
death called
and took you all away from me

- i miss you all more than you will ever know

it all started out
with hugs in airports
we had vegan donuts
and walked around a park
that was central
we ran through the rain
and looked for missing trains
we spun around
on sea glass carousels
and our smiles
were just as bright
as those city lights

- the night before enchanted

sitting with you
in your car
in my driveway
with our hands intertwined
was my favorite part
of that summer

- summer 2016

i have a fire burning inside of me
how dare you try to put it out
you can not put out my flames
or my wildfire mind
or the embers in my stomach

- heart of an aries

there was a time in my life
where i felt so alone
even when surrounded by others
i was convinced no one cared
even when the few people that seemed to
told me they did
i could never believe it
i spent every night
crying myself to sleep
wanting it to end
i needed something
that would convince me to stay
and right when i needed it
i was told that it does get better

- and guess what? it is starting to

there are so many times where
i have been the girl in the middle
the girl who comes after that girl
that tragically broke that guys heart
i am also the girl that comes before
the new girl he actually wants
i am just always there
to pass by his time
and now looking back at it
i should have saved my time for someone
who was actually worth mine

anxiety and depression are the monsters under my bed
like from when i was a kid
i try to keep them hidden
i do everything to ignore them
to stop them from coming out
and when they do it consumes me
it is like they are pulling me back under with them
and i have no way to stop them

i found my new favorite ring in your city
the new city you call home
i walked around and stumbled upon a shop
and it became my new favorite ring
my new favorite thing from your city
and now this ring will be the greatest thing i ever got out of that visit

- i never needed you anyway

out with the old and in with the new
just as you seem to always do
you manage to attach yourself
to the newest and latest friend
and then you stab them in the back in the end

they always say home is not a place
and that home is really a feeling
i was not sure if this was true
but then i felt at home, when i was with all of you

- to my real friends

we were built
just as sandcastles were
we were crafted so beautifully
and every part carved out
and fit just right
but the waves got taller
and faster
and stronger
and angrier
and the little sandcastle that was us
got washed away with everything else

- we were never strong enough to handle oceans

do you twirl your hair when you are anxious
and hold your breath when asked questions about yourself
even if it is the smallest "how are you?"
because you are scared of talking too much or for too long
do you understand what it is like to bite your tongue
for everything you have ever wanted to say
but hesitated because you know that
these people do not want to hear it anyway
do you realize what it is like
to not be able to get up out of bed
do you know what it is like
to wish you had a desire to be alive

- i wish i was anyone but myself

i have so much love
begging and knocking on my heart
to be set free and to love someone
but no one ever wants my love
so it will stay locked away
until hopefully one day
someone shows up with the key
that will open up my heart
and release all my love to them

the ocean was my safe place
to look out
and not know what is beyond the sea
to look and see nothing
but waves
is just so calming to me

i remember looking around
at all of the flashing lights
and just letting time stop for for a moment
and i shut my eyes
to spin around
to take it all in
i held my breath
and then opened my eyes
and i reminded myself
i need to remember how i feel now
in this moment
for the rest of my life

- summer 2018

i spent the worse half of the last year
researching medications
and looking through my own medicine cabinet
i was so desperate to find something
to make it all stop

your twisted tongue
and your toxic words
are going to get you in far worse trouble
than your loss of a friendship with me
there are going to be people
that will drag you to pieces
even further than i did
so when all these things catch up to you
do not come crying to me
or anyone
you have no one to blame but yourself
and one day when this bites you in the ass
oh and it will
i can promise you that
do not say i did not warn you
because i did sweetie.

my whole life
i always wondered
what having a sister was like
to know there is someone
always there, whenever you needed to shed a tear
i always wondered
what having someone to lean on was like
i learned that sisters
are not bound by blood
and i discovered
the sister i had always wanted
was right here

- to my big sister

the moments
when you feel safe
and at home
in the hugs of your friends
that live miles away
you live in the moments
of flashing lights
and bright lights
and confetti
that never stops coming down
in group hugs
in front of flower walls
and matching socks
and rivers with
jumping kayaks
and confetti
that just
never seems to stop
pouring down

- nashville

i have learned
that some people are worth forgiving
sometimes it is easier to move on from the past
forgive but never forget
but just because you forgave one person
does not mean you have to forgive them all

there was something about the way this city
was able to hold so much magic
captured in the middle of tall buildings
maybe it was the warming hugs
i had with my friends
when meeting them for the first time
maybe it was the reunion outside the hotel
and the walks in the park that brought us to wonderland
maybe it was the long chat in a juice bar
filled with lemonade and polaroids
maybe it was the late night hotel talks
that made me laugh just enough to spill my wine

- new york, 2019

i found freedom on a plane to LA
and coffee shops in my town
and the sinking feeling of knowing
i can not really count on people anyway
if i ever wanted to live a life so free
i had to take the first step to do so
far away from my social anxiety

you had me on mute
but sweetheart
that is not what friends do

- did you think i would not find out?

i put so much into friendships
wondering when what i put in
would return for me
i searched for signs of good friendship
in people that would never even show up for me
i realized that not everything we do in this life
will be guaranteed to return to us
so i decided to still show up anyway
i still cared for all the people
who never even thought twice about me
i tried my best to make sure no one else
knew what it felt like to feel so forgotten

i still remember
the sour taste
you left on my lips
when i knew that would be
our final kiss

i found my closure in one last batch of sprinkled sugar cookies
and realizing that i did everything i could
to be the very best friend i could be

- but nothing would ever be enough

there have been so many moments
with the right people
in the right places
that remind me
no matter how much i think i am
i will never truly be alone
and that feeling
truly feels like home

the sad thing is
you will forever be incapable of seeing
how you really treat people
you will always and only
be thinking of yourself

she was surrounded by loss
and leaves that fell off trees
her thoughts echoed "it will never get better"
she was convinced this was her life
and that this was it
she saw no light or reason to keep going
she managed to hit rock bottom
and kept digging herself down
if only she knew that one day
she would wake up and get on a plane
walk around a big, bright and loud city
and finally feel free

i am haunted with the days of my past
anytime i would talk
you never actually listened
anytime i would vent
you never actually listened
it has been so many years now
yet this still lurks in my mind
you choosing not to listen
caused me to choose to never speak again

the general rule of life
has no schedule you must stick to
there is no race
no prize for being first
no winners or losers
there is no way to fall behind
or anyway to get ahead
we are all just learning
to get along
to live our lives
in the best way possible
there is no destination
that we have to get to

- you are doing exactly what you are meant to be doing

you cut me down
on more than one occasion
you used how much i valued our friendship against me
i could never express how i felt
or what upset me
without you running away
and hiding from me
my caring heart has gotten me into
a lot of trouble since those days
but instead of voicing what upsets me now
i decide to just shove it back down

i started putting on red lipstick at the age of 14
i looked for every dress that i thought fit just right
i straightened my hair everyday until it turned to straw
i did my makeup just to cry it off at the end of the night
i spent everyday looking for a photo opportunity
i searched for self love behind a camera
i got lost in comparison
they tell us we have to learn to love ourselves
then tell us the most critical person
we will ever encounter, is also ourselves

- i am still trying to find a world in which i feel beautiful

you would threaten to walk away
anytime i mentioned how something
you did, upset me
i started to panic
and would confront you less and less
only causing me to hurt more and more
in fear of losing you from my life
i kept all of it inside
you managed to keep me in my place
by trying to control what upset me
this caused me to never know
if what i was feeling was rational or not

- i still do not know what i am allowed to be upset over

i can not wait
for the day
that you find your own soulmate
and you will and when you do
trust me you will feel it in your bones
it will feel almost like
it was meant to be
almost like
it was your destiny

there is something
so calming about the sound of rain
as you lay there at 2am
hearing the gentle sound of it hitting the roof of your house
and then theres a shake and a boom of thunder
that takes you away from being lost in the rain
it reminds you that this storm will not last forever
and neither will yours

she took one last look around
one quick glance
before she drove away
the trees and the grass
may look normal
to almost anyone else
but to her they were memory filled
she can still picture the old swing set
and the years of summers spent in the pool
she remembers the colors of the trees
when october came around
she remembered the snowfalls
that covered the lawn in the coldest of winters
and all the christmas lights that hung
and the time spring finally rolled around
and the afternoons were spent
chasing all the migrating butterflies

- memory lane

the run rises
the sun sets
old endings
new beginnings

Acknowledgements

For starters i am so lucky to have had people in my life who checked in on me, cared for me, and helped me heal over the past couple of years. I know who my true friends are, and will never forget who stuck around when my world came crashing down. You know who you are.

My mom - Thank you for always coming to my rescue, and running away with me to chicago or new york or nashville or toronto or florida whenever I need it. Thank you for shaping me into the person I am today and showing me all the love in the world.

My dad - Thank you for inspiring me to chase my dreams and live my life to the fullest and always doing everything you can to give me the best things in this life.

Patricia - You were the first person I ever shared any of my poems with, you know about these poems better than anyone, you lived through all of these moments with me. Thank you for encouraging me, and supporting me always and sticking around all these years.

Kristina - You showed up for me in so many different ways and so many different times. Thank you for being my big sister, for making me feel understood, for listening to me and for helping me through the most difficult times in my life and for helping me get my voice back and encouraging me to speak up.

Taylor - Thank you for always going out of your way to make me feel special. I feel so lucky to know you and to have such a fantastic and thoughtful friend in my life, thank you for making me feel so loved and cared for.

Destiny - I am forever thankful for the summer that made us such close friends. Thank you for reminding me of who I am and what I am capable of and giving me the best advice that I can always look back on. Thank you for caring and inspiring me everyday, and always telling me exactly what I need to hear.

Joren - Thank you for always being only one phone call away even though we are a 5 hour plane ride away, thank you for being my rock and listening to my voice memo rants and always being the person I can come to.

Thank you to anyone who bought this book.
Thank you to anyone who shared it on social media.
Thank you to anyone who has ever read anything of mine.
Thank you to the people who inspired every single one of these poems.
Thank you to the people who told me my poems were inspiring.
Thank you to the people who wanted to print my words out.
Thank you to anyone who cared enough about me to help me feel heard.
Thank you to anyone who believed in me.

Until next time… thank you.

About the author
Kassandra Olschanski is 21 years old and lives in Michigan.
She is currently pursuing a degree in Political Science.
This is her first poetry book and she is in the process of creating her
second one.

Social Media
Instagram: kassaandra13
Twitter: kassandrasmagic

CPSIA information can be obtained
at www.ICGtesting.com
Printed in the USA
LVHW091525250420
654414LV00004B/1532

9 781097 678945